KU-685-519

Contents

The finest playwright

William Shakespeare wrote what is probably the finest poetry and certainly the finest plays ever to appear in English. Many believe his plays are the best ever written in any language.

This claim rests upon the evidence of thirty-seven plays, four long poems and 154 fourteen-line poems known as 'sonnets'. All of these works were almost certainly written between 1588 and 1613.

The greatness of William Shakespeare's work does not depend upon its subject matter. The main theme of the sonnets is love – hardly an original subject for poetry. Moreover, most of the plays are re-workings of old stories that were well known in Shakespeare's day. A play about a Prince Hamlet of Denmark, for instance, had been presented on the London stage in 1589, some twelve years before Shakespeare wrote his own immortal version.

Shakespeare is most famous for his plays. Three qualities make them unique: the range of memorable characters, the beauty of much of their language, and, most outstanding of all, the light that each throws on the pleasures and problems of human existence.

TO THE READER.

Portrait of genius? This engraved picture of William Shakespeare that was printed in the first full collection of his works in 1623 is probably the best likeness we have.

The modern Globe Theatre, Southwark, London, is a close copy of that in which many of Shakespeare's most famous plays were first performed.

Even today, almost four hundred years since Shakespeare's death, **audiences** leave a Shakespeare play feeling that they have witnessed something modern, something relevant to their own lives.

Shadowy genius

It is, however, much easier to say what Shakespeare did than who he was. About the man himself surprisingly little is known. There are two reasons for this. The first is that he did not belong to the class of 'important persons' – monarchs, high clergymen and the nobility – who dominated society. At the time, the life of a playwright, however successful and respected, was not considered worth recording in detail. The second is that Shakespeare's plays give us very few clues about his personal thoughts and feelings. His characters are independent beings, not shadows of their creator. For this reason scholars have claimed that Shakespeare was, variously, Roman Catholic, Protestant, extremist, **conservative** and so forth. The truth is, we have very little detailed information about what sort of man he was – other than an outstanding genius.

How do we know?

There are two types of source about Shakespeare and his times. Most plentiful are secondary sources. These are books, articles, videos, websites and so on that have been produced by people who have studied that period.

Primary sources, on the other hand, come from Shakespeare's own day and include anything that can throw light on that time. Some are physical objects, ranging from buildings to drinking mugs. By excavating the remains of the old Rose Theatre in London, for example, scholars learned about the size and shape of theatres in Shakespeare's time.

The most useful primary sources on Shakespeare himself are hand-written or printed **documents** from the sixteenth or seventeenth centuries. These should be approached with care, however, as his own plays throw only an uncertain light on the character and ideas of the writer. Furthermore, none of them (see page 48) exist in his own handwriting. There are even those who believe the works we attribute to William Shakespeare were in fact written by someone else!

The early printed texts, as we shall see (page 48), are often full of mistakes and confusions. None of the playwright's letters have survived. We have only one picture of him, and even that may not be accurate. The most personal document we have is his will (see page 47). We are obliged, therefore, to piece together Shakespeare's biography by using official documents, snippets of information and the recorded memories of those who knew him, or, like Thomas Betterton (see page 9), had spoken with those who knew him.

Born in 1564, Shakespeare lived mostly during the reign of Queen Elizabeth I (1558-1603), the last of the Tudor monarchs. Fortunately, the range of primary sources for Elizabethan times is large, making it quite easy for us to fill in the general background to Shakespeare's life. There is less material on the Elizabethan theatre. We have only one picture of actors on stage, for instance. We do not know what some theatres looked like.

England's Queen Elizabeth I (1558–1603) was one of Shakespeare's most influential admirers. This portrait was painted after her navy's defeat of the Spanish Armada (1588).

Finally, there is the problem of language. The English of Shakespeare and his contemporaries was very similar to ours, but not exactly the same. By 'nice', for example, Shakespeare meant 'having loose morals', not 'pleasant'. As a result, Elizabethan English can be a little confusing to those meeting it for the first time.

7

Birth of a genius

William was the first son of John and Mary Shakespeare, a middle-class couple from the market town of Stratford-upon-Avon, about 160 kilometres (100 miles) north-west of London. He must have been born before Wednesday, 26 April 1564, for on that day his parents saw him baptised in the local parish church, Holy Trinity.

Tradition says William was born on 23 April, a date of double significance. It is the day on which he died and, appropriately enough, the name day of St George, England's **patron saint**.

The Shakespeares were a well-heeled and respected couple. William's mother was one of the Ardens, a family that had owned land in Warwickshire for generations. Her husband also came from farming stock but had given up the land to establish a successful business making high-quality leather goods, such as gloves and belts.

William was probably born in the family home in Henley Street, which, although much altered, still stands. Two elder sisters died in infancy and he grew up with three younger brothers – Gilbert, Edmund and Richard – and a younger sister, Joan.

An old drawing, now in the British Museum, showing the house in Stratford-upon-Avon in which William Shakespeare was born in 1564.

First biography

In 1709 Nicholas Rowe produced the first carefully **edited** edition of William Shakespeare's works. In his introduction he included stories of the playwright's life collected in Stratford by the actor Thomas Betterton. Rowe's 'note' is the first biography of William Shakespeare.

He was the son of Mr John Shakespeare, and was born at Stratford-upon-Avon, in Warwickshire, in April 1564. His family, as appears by the register and publick writings relating to that town, were of good figure and fashion there, and are mentioned as gentlemen. His father, who was a considerable dealer in wool, had so large a family, ten children in all, that though he was the eldest son, he could give him no better education than his own employment.

The citizens

Writing in 1600, when William was thirty-six, Sir Thomas Wilson divided the population into social classes and described each in turn. Here he describes those he called the 'Citizens', the **urban** middle classes like the Shakespeares.

These, by reason of the great privileges they enjoy, every city being, as it were, a commonwealth [independent state] among themselves, no other officer of the Queen nor other having authority to intermeddle amongst them, must needs be exceeding well to pass [well-to-do]. They are not taxed but by their own officers of the[ir] own brotherhood, every art [profession] having one or two of his own which are continually of the **council** of the city in all affairs to see that nothing pass to the contrary to their profit. ...[In Norwich] I have known in my time 24 aldermen [town councillors] which were esteemed to be worth £20,000 apiece, some much more...

Shakespeare's England

William was born into a population of about 3 million people, ten per cent of whom lived in towns. London, where he would spend much of his life, was the only large city (see pages 20-21).

Society was dominated by a handful of wealthy, **titled** families. People of the 'middling sort', like the Shakespeares, were no more than a few hundred thousand. The majority of Elizabethans lived short lives on the edge of poverty.

People's lives centred around their locality: the parish and the county. They had little to do with central government and it had little to do with them. Even so, Queen Elizabeth wielded considerable authority. She was advised by a **council** of her own choosing and a parliament that met when she wished. A wise monarch, however, kept in with at least some of the great families.

Religion, much more important then than it is in today's society, focused on the Protestant Church of England (re-founded 1559). Its archbishops, bishops and priests were Elizabeth's only network of paid local **civil servants**.

A well-dressed couple ride to market. Almost all inland journeys were taken on horseback or on foot along rough and often dangerous roads.

Three sorts of poor

In the 1570s, during William's boyhood, the **Puritan** clergyman and scholar William Harrison (1535-93) compiled a remarkable 'Description of England'. It was printed in 1577. In this extract he describes the ever-present poor.

There was no mercy for 'sturdy beggars' who, it was believed, chose not to work: this pair were tied together and whipped out of town.

With us the poor is commonly divided into three sorts, so that some are poor by impotency, as [such as] the fatherless child, the aged, blind, and lame, and the diseased person that is judged incurable; the second are poor by casualty, as the wounded soldier, the decayed householder, and the sick person visited with grievous and painful diseases; the third consisteth of the thriftless [taking no care] poor, as the rioter that hath consumed all, the vagabond that will abide nowhere but runneth up and down from place to place (as it were seeking work and finding none), and finally, the rogue and strumpet [prostitute], which are not possible to be divided in sunder [separated] but run to and fro over all the realm, chiefly keeping the champaign [open] soils in summer to avoid the scorching heat, and the woodland grounds in winter to eschew [avoid] the blustering winds.

For the first two sorts ... which are the true poor indeed and for whom the Word [the Bible] doth bind us to make some daily provision, there is order taken throughout every parish in the realm that weekly collection shall be made for their help and sustenation [support], to the end [so] they should not scatter abroad and, by begging here and there, annoy both town and country.

Stratford and school

The inhabitants of Stratford-upon-Avon were only a five-minute walk from the sights and scents of the rich Warwickshire countryside. Moreover, as it was a market town, there were always interesting travellers passing through.

The young William almost certainly saw dramatic presentations, including local performances of traditional English **morality plays**. There were also foreign **players** offering Commedia dell' Arte, the latest dramatic fashion in continental Europe.

As the son of one of Stratford's more important citizens – John Shakespeare played an active part in town government – William must have attended the local grammar school. Here, having already learned how to read and write, he would have studied arithmetic and the Classics (Latin and Greek).

Classical knowledge was an essential part of Elizabethan education and William's writing is full of allusion to the ancient culture. Interestingly, however, Ben Jonson noted that William – perhaps because he left school early – knew 'small [little] Latin, and less Greek'. Some scholars believe this was a blessing in disguise as it left his mind uncluttered by old styles and conventions.

An artist's impression of what Stratford's grammar school may have been like in Shakespeare's time. We assume he went to this school, but we have no proof.

A brief life
John Aubrey (1626-97) had an **amateur** interest in all aspects of the past and in the lives of those of his own time. His amusing *Brief Lives*, written in the 1680s, is full of quirky details.

Mr William Shakespeare was born at Stratford upon Avon in the County of Warwick. His father was a butcher, and I have been told heretofore [previously, beforehand] by some of the neighbours, that when he was a boy he exercised his father's Trade, but when he kill'd a Calfe he would doe it in high style, and make a Speech. There was at this time another Butcher's son in this Towne that was held not at all inferior to him for a naturall witt, his acquaintance and coetanean [**contemporary**], but died young.

This William, being inclined naturally to Poetry and acting, came to London, I guess about 18: and was an Actor at one of the **play-houses**, and did exceedingly well: now B. Johnson was never a good Actor but an excellent Instructor.

He began early to make essays at Dramatique Poetry, which at that time was very low; and his plays tooke well.

He was a handsome, well-shap't man: very good company, and of a very readie and pleasant smoothe Witt.

Faith and the Church of England

Around 1576 John Shakespeare ran into financial difficulties. He sold property and was fined for not attending church at a law court. Later, in 1592, he was reprimanded for not going to church. Some scholars suggest that these incidents show that he was a Roman Catholic.

During the reign of Henry VIII (1509–47), at the start of the English **Reformation**, England had broken with the Pope but remained largely Catholic. During the next two reigns the country's official religion swung first to Protestantism, then back to Catholicism. Many people, such as Cicely Ormes, below, were killed because of their religious beliefs.

When Elizabeth I became queen in 1558, she established a **compromise** Protestant Church of England with herself as its Supreme Governor. Although she did not want 'to make a window into men's souls', she could not accept open dissent.

The Queen executed some three hundred Roman Catholics for owing **allegiance** to a foreign power – the pope. Other Roman Catholics were heavily fined for not attending church. Was one of these John Shakespeare? And might William have followed in his father's faith?

An age of intolerance: the Protestant woman Cicely Ormes is burned alive for heresy during the reign of Elizabeth's Roman Catholic sister, Mary I (1553–8).

His shirt was made long down to his feet, which were bare; and
his head ... was so bare that not one hair could be seen upon it.
His beard was long and thick, covering his face with marvellous
gravity. Such a countenance [face, impression] of gravity moved
the hearts both of his friends and enemies.

Then an iron chain was tied about Cranmer, and ... they
commanded the fire to be set to him. And when the wood was
kindled, and the fire began to burn near him, stretching out his
arm, he put his right hand into the flame, which he held so
steadfast and immovable that all men might see his hand
burned before his body was touched.* His body did so abide the
burning of the flame with such constancy and steadfastness,
that standing always in one place, without moving his body, he
seemed to move no more than the stake to which he was bound;
his eyes were lifted up to heaven, and oftentimes he repeated,
'This unworthy right hand!' so long as his voice would suffer
him; and using often the words of Stephen, 'Lord Jesus receive
my spirit!' in the greatness of the flame he gave up the ghost.

* Cranmer had previously used this hand to sign a renunciation of
his Protestant faith, a move which he now regretted.

A Renaissance state

William Shakespeare thrived on the tensions and liveliness of Elizabethan England – a bustling, confident and aggressive little state not too limited by custom or convention. For 200 years an intellectual change had been moving from Italy slowly northwest across Europe. It impacted upon the arts and learning and led people to think more highly of individual human beings. We call this movement the Renaissance.

A fresh interest in classical learning, including plays in Latin and Greek, marked the Renaissance. By the 1560s English dramas based on Classical originals appeared. Then came short one-act plays – interludes – that combined native English and classical themes. In the 1570s purpose-built **playhouses** appeared.

The famous sketch of London's Swan Playhouse (1596) by the Dutchman Johann de Witt is the only **contemporary** illustration of the inside of an Elizabethan theatre.

By the next decade a distinctively English style of **professional** theatre was emerging in London – just when the young William Shakespeare came to town. The form of English that he used was relatively new and it was largely due to him that dramatic writing in English was accepted as literature.

The argument of tragedies is wrath, cruelty, incest, injury, murder either
violent by sword, or voluntary by poison. The persons, Gods, Goddesses,
juries, friends, Kings, Queens, and mighty men. The ground work of
Comedies, is love, cozenage [deceit], flattery, bawdry [dirtiness, smut],
sly conveyance of whoredom; the persons, cooks, knaves, bawds, parasites,
courtesans [loose women], lecherous old men, amorous young men ...

Sometimes you shall see nothing but the adventures of an amorous
knight passing from country to country for the love of his lady,
encountering many a terrible monster made of brown paper, and at his
return is so wonderfully changed, that he cannot be known but by some
posy in his tablet, or by a broken ring, or a handkerchief, or a piece of
cockle shell, what learn you by that? When the soul of your plays is
either mere trifles or Italian bawdry, or cussing of gentlewomen, what
are we taught? ...

The ancient Philosophers ... called them a monster of many heads ... The
common people which resort to Theatres being but an assembly of
Tailors, Tinkers, Cordwainers [rope makers], Sailors, Old men, young
men, Women, Boys, Girls and the such like ...

So in Comedies delight being moved with variety of shows, of events, of
music, the longer we gaze, the more we crave ...

Marriage and mystery

Early sources say William worked for his father after leaving school and Aubrey (see page 13) says he spent some time as a schoolmaster. Both may be correct. However, it is not until 1582 that we know for certain what he was doing.

In November that year the eighteen-year-old William married Anne Hathaway, the twenty-six-year-old daughter of a local farmer. She was three months pregnant and her first child, Susanna, was born the following May. Twins, Hamnet and Judith, followed early in 1585.

Anne and William lived with his parents. What he thought of this arrangement we don't know, but he probably did not enjoy it: the next time we know for certain where he was, he was not in Stratford at all.

A rather fanciful Victorian picture of what the interior of Anne Hathaway's Cottage may have looked like in the sixteenth century.

Rowe says William left home because, having fallen in with 'ill company' he was in trouble with Sir Thomas Lucy. Others believe he had joined a **troupe** of travelling actors. Whatever the reason, by 1592 William Shakespeare was living in London.

A Woman Moved...

Scholars have often wondered about the relationship between William and Anne. In *The Taming of the Shrew* (1593–4) the newly married Kate explains a wife's duty in marriage. Perhaps this extremely anti-feminist speech was wishful thinking on William's part – or is it ironic?

A women moved is like a fountain troubled,
Muddy, ill-seeming, thick, bereft of [without] beauty,
And while it is so, none so dry or thirsty
Will deign [agree] to sip or touch one drop of it.
Thy husband is thy lord, thy life, thy keeper,
Thy head, thy sovereign – one that cares for thee,
And for thy maintenance commits his body
To painful labour both by sea and land,
To watch the night in storms, the day in cold,
Whilst thou li'st warm at home, secure and safe;
And craves no other tribute at thy hands
But love, fair looks, and true obedience:
Too little payment for so great a debt.
Such duty as the subject owes the prince,
Even such a woman oweth to her husband,
And when she is froward, [unreasonable]
    peevish, sullen, sour,
And not obedient to his honest will,
What is she but a foul contending rebel
And graceless traitor to her loving lord?
I am ashamed that women are so simple
To offer war where they should kneel for peace,
Or seek for rule, supremacy, and sway,
When they are bound to serve, love, and obey.

Shakespeare's London

London, where the young William Shakespeare came in the later 1580s, was England's only great city. With a population approaching 200,000, it was the country's political, economic, social and artistic capital.

The original walled City lay on the north bank of the Thames. Dominated by the ancient St Paul's Cathedral and the Tower of London, it was a thriving port and centre for every sort of business. Its size and enormous wealth attracted shady characters of every sort.

By Shakespeare's time, buildings had now spilled way beyond the old walls. To the west they stretched along the Strand to the royal palaces of Whitehall and Westminster. London Bridge linked with the Thames' south bank, and housing sprawled beyond the gates to the north and east.

The city government of elected mayor and **corporation** lived in constant fear of the unruly mob. But their rule ran only within the walls. Beyond, especially to the south, Londoners breathed a freer air – and here, in Southwark, William Shakespeare would make his name.

Shakespeare's London: an imagined view of London Bridge. Passing beneath the bridge in a boat was a dangerous business.

Two Publique Houses

John Stow (1525-1605), a member of the City of London Merchant Taylors Company, published a famous *Survey of London* in 1598. In this passage about the expansion of London north of the walls he mentions the Theatre, where William first worked on coming to the capital.

From Aldgate east again lieth a large street, replenished with buildings; to wit [i.e.], on the north side of the parish church of St Botolph, and so other buildings, to Hog Lane, and to the bars on both sides.

Also, without [outside] the bars [moveable barriers across the road] both the sides of the street be pestered with cottages and alleys, even up to Whitechapel church, and almost half a mile beyond it, into the common field ...

North, and by east from Bishopsgate, lieth a large street or highway, having on the west side thereof the parish church of St Botolph.

Then is the hospital of St Mary of Bethelem, founded by a citizen of London... [and] thence up to the late dissolved priory of St John Baptist, called Holywell, a house of nuns, of old time, founded by a bishop of London ... The church thereof being pulled down, many houses have been built for the lodgings of noblemen, of strangers born, and other. And near thereunto are builded two publique houses for the acting and shewe of comedies, tragedies, and histories, for recreation. Whereof one is called the Courtein, [Curtain] the other the Theatre; both standing on the south-west side of the field.

Young man at the theatre

In 1592, in the first reference to William in London, the playwright Robert Greene wrote a piece attacking him as 'an **upstart** Crow'. Later that year we hear that the three parts of *Henry VI*, which William helped write, were enormously popular. Perhaps earlier, he wrote *The Comedy of Errors*, adapted from a play by the Roman writer Plautus.

Before turning to writing William may have helped at the theatre or, more likely, worked as an actor of small parts and then helped out by writing a line or two. When fellow actors saw the merit of these lines, he may have been asked to do more until he was writing whole plays.

Playwriting was then a new and not very well-regarded skill. Indeed, before the arrival of William and his great **contemporary**, Christopher Marlowe (1564-93), most English drama was written in poor-quality **verse** (called doggerel). It was common for plays to be put together by several writers and then altered by the actors.

Shakespeare in rehearsal: an imaginary picture of what the interior of the Globe **Playhouse** may have looked like.

Shakespeare's boys
The great eighteenth-century literary figure Dr Samuel Johnson (1709-94) told this story (which originated with Rowe) about William's first job in London.

In the time of Elizabeth, coaches being yet uncommon, and hired coaches not at all in use, those who were too proud, too tender, or too idle to walk, went on horseback to any distant business or diversion. Many came on horseback to the play, and when Shakespeare fled to London from the terror of criminal prosecution [a reference to the story that William fled to London to escape Sir Thomas Lucy], his first expedient was to wait at the door of the play-house, and hold the horses of those that had no servants, that they might be ready again after the performance. In this office [job] he became so conspicuous for his care and readiness, that in a very short time every man as he alighted (his horse) called for Will. Shakespeare, and scarcely any other waiter was trusted with a horse while Will. Shakespeare could be had.

This was the first dawn of better fortune. Shakespeare, finding more horses put into his hand than he could hold, hired boys to wait under his inspection, who when Will. Shakespeare was summoned, were immediately to present themselves [call out these words], I am Shakespeare's boy, Sir. In time Shakespeare found higher employment, but as long as the practice of riding to the play-house continued, the waiters that held horses retained the appellation [name] of Shakespeare's boys.

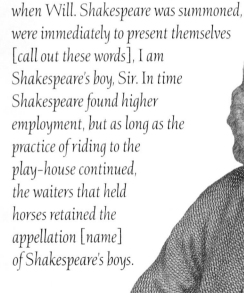

Dr Samuel Johnson, the eighteenth-century writer who retold stories about Shakespeare's mysterious early life.

Plague and patronage

Scholars date several of William's plays from the early 1590s: *Titus Andronicus*, *Love's Labours Lost*, and two new plays about English history, *King John* and *Richard III*. In the latter William reached new heights of poetry and drama, and, with the wicked king, produced his first truly memorable stage character.

Then, disaster. A violent outbreak of **bubonic plague** struck London towards the end of 1592 and the authorities banned all large gatherings of people at which the disease could be spread. The theatres were closed.

Needing employment, William turned to Henry Wriothesley, the young **Earl** of Southampton, who had noted the playwright's talent. Perhaps receiving as much as £1000 in return, William wrote two long poems – *Venus and Adonis* (1593) and *The Rape of Lucrece* (1594) – and dedicated them to his young **patron**. Both poems were printed immediately. At the same time he began writing his brilliant series of 154 fourteen-line **sonnets** that were eventually printed in 1609.

The immortal patron: Henry Wriothesley, 3rd Earl of Southampton, who is principally remembered for his patronage of the young Shakespeare.

Across the bridge
By the 1590s a third **playhouse**, the Rose, had been built, this time on the south bank of the Thames. As the German visitor Lupold von Wedel tells us, Londoners were used to Southwark as a place of lively entertainment.

Blood-sports Elizabethan style – bear baiting, involving savage dogs fighting with a chained bear, was immensely popular.

The Thames is crossed by a bridge, leading to another town on the other side of the water called Sedorck [Southwark]...

On 23rd we went across the bridge to the above-mentioned town. There is a round building three stories high, in which are kept about a hundred large English dogs, with separate wooden kennels for each of them. These dogs were made to fight singly with three bears... After this a horse was brought in and chased by the dogs, and at last a bull, who defended himself very bravely. The next was that a number of men and women came forward from a separate compartment, dancing, conversing, and fighting with each other; also a man who threw some white bread among the crowd, that it might scramble for it. Right over the middle of the place a rose was fixed, this rose being set on fire by a rocket: suddenly lots of apples and pears fell out of it down upon the people standing below. While the people were scrambling for the apples, some rockets were made to fall down upon them out of the rose, which caused a great fright but amused the spectators. After this, rockets and other fireworks came flying out of all corners, and that was the end of the play.

The Lord Chamberlain's Men

Elizabethan plays were staged by companies of actors, writers and businessmen. We don't know for which company William worked before the **bubonic plague**, but in 1594 he joined the up-and-coming actor Richard Burbage (c.1567-1619) to form a company under the **patronage** of the **Lord Chamberlain**, Henry Carey, Lord Hunsdon.

The Lord Chamberlain's Men used the Theatre **playhouse** until 1596. More significantly, they were also staging plays elsewhere: starting with a performance at Greenwich in 1594, they regularly appeared at court (see pages 28 and 38).

Now in his thirties, William's style and technique were maturing fast. In the mid-1590s he wrote four truly great plays: *Romeo and Juliet* and *A Midsummer Night's Dream* (both 1594-6), *Richard II* (1595) and *The Merchant of Venice* (1596-7). Their variety, the richness of their language, their dramatic skill and, above all, their profound understanding of what it is to be a human being were startling: nothing like it had ever before been seen on the English stage.

Eternally popular – a modern production of *Romeo and Juliet* with Clare Danes as the 'star-struck' lover Juliet.

A petition

In 1596, the lease on the Theatre ran out and the Lord Chamberlain's Men were looking for an alternative venue. They bought a hall at Blackfriars within the City walls but local residents successfully petitioned against its use as a theatre.

One Burbage hath lately bought certain rooms in the precinct near adjoining unto the dwelling houses of the right honourable the Lord Chamberlain and the Lord of Hunsdon, which rooms the said Burbage is now altering and meaneth very shortly to convert and turn the same into a common playhouse, which will grow to be a very great annoyance and trouble, not only to all the noblemen and gentlemen thereabout inhabiting but also a general inconvenience to all the inhabitants of the same precinct, both by reason of the great resort and gathering together of all manner of vagrant [vagabond] and lewd [immoral] persons that, under colour of resorting to plays, will come thither and work all manner of mischief, and also to the great pestering and filling up of the same precincts, if it should please God to send any visitation of sickness as heretofore hath been, [a reference to the recent outbreak of the plague] for that the same precinct is already grown very populous; and besides, that the same playhouse is so near the Church that the noise of the drums and trumpets will greatly disturb and hinder both the ministers and parishioners in time of divine service and sermons...

27

At court

The royal court – meaning both the monarch and courtiers, and the place where they met – was at the heart of English political, social and artistic life. The courts of William's monarchs – Elizabeth I and her Scottish cousin James I (1603-25) – often spent Christmas in Whitehall Palace, London. During the rest of the year they moved between palaces near the capital, such as Hampton Court, Greenwich and Windsor.

At court gathered the leading politicians, churchmen, nobles, merchants and – if they were lucky – artists, musicians and writers. A playwright's highest success was to have work performed at court. The **Lord Chamberlain's** Men appeared at Elizabeth's court more than any other company. It is even said that William wrote *The Merry Wives of Windsor* at the Queen's special command.

Under James I William's links with the court would become even closer. James took over as company **patron**, renaming it the King's Men. The tragedy *Macbeth* (about 1605) was written specifically to please the new king (see page 38).

Sir John Falstaff, one of Shakespeare's most famous creations, hides in a basket of filthy laundry in *The Merry Wives of Windsor*.

Attending the court

The most lively description of court theatre in William's time comes from the Venetian Orazio Busino. He wrote it after attending the court of King James during Christmas 1617–18.

... there was such a crowd; for though they claim to admit only those favoured with invitations, nevertheless every box was full, especially with most noble and richly dressed ladies, 600 and more in number, according to the general opinion; their clothes of such various styles and colours as to be indescribable...

...At about the 6th hour of the night his majesty appeared with his court, having passed through the apartments where the ambassadors were waiting... As he entered the hall fifteen or twenty cornets and trumpets began to play, antiphonally [in musical parts] and very well. After his majesty had been seated under the canopy alone, the Queen not being present because of some indisposition, he had the ambassadors sit on two stools, and the great officers and the magistrates sat on benches. The Lord Chamberlain then had the way cleared, and in the middle of the room there appeared a fine and spacious area all covered with green cloth. A large curtain – painted to represent a tent of gold with a broad fringe, the background of blue canvas flecked all over with golden stars – was made to fall in an instant. This concealed the stage ...

Royal command: an imaginary scene in which Queen Elizabeth I enjoys a play specially performed before her at the court.

29

This scept'red isle

William lived at a significant time in English history. England was developing into a 'nation state' – an independent country with a common language, government, culture and heritage. Today almost everyone lives in such a state, but that was not the case in William's day.

Before the **Reformation**, when the Protestants split from the Roman Catholic church (see page 10), all Western Europeans belonged to 'Christendom', the international Christian community. Much of Europe owed **allegiance**, in theory, to an elected ruler known as the **Holy Roman Emperor**. The modern countries of Germany and Italy were just names for collections of states.

This England
In *Richard II*, the old warrior John of Gaunt lies on his deathbed and complains how his native England has been betrayed by a weak king. The speech is perhaps the most poetic piece of English patriotism ever penned.

Gradually, out of this patchwork, individual nations were emerging. England, Scotland and France were among the first. And with the nation state came a new sentiment: patriotism, or love of the homeland. It swept England in 1588, when a Spanish invasion fleet – the Armada – was defeated. In tune with the times, William reflected the new patriotism in two of his plays, *Richard II* and *Henry V* (1599).

Rule Britannia! A 20th-century painting of a dramatic scene during the defeat of the Spanish Armada, 1588.

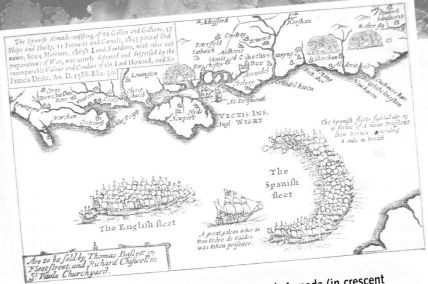

An ancient drawing of the Spanish Armada (in crescent formation) sailing up the Channel towards Calais, where it planned to collect troops for an invasion of England.

Methinks I am a prophet new inspired,
And thus expiring do foretell of him
    [the king, Richard II]:
His rash fierce blaze of riot cannot last,
For violent fires soon burn out themselves.
Small showers last long, but sudden storms
    are short;
He tires betimes [quickly] that spurs too
    fast betimes;
With eager feeding, food doth choke the
    feeder.
Light vanity, insatiate cormorant,
Consuming means, soon preys upon itself.
This royal throne of kings, this scept'red
    isle,
This earth of majesty, this seat of Mars
    [the Roman god of war],
This other Eden, demi-paradise,
This fortress built by Nature for herself
Against infection and the hand of war,
This happy breed of men, this little world,
This precious stone set in a silver sea

Which serves it in the office of a wall,
Or as a moat defensive to a house,
Against the envy of less happier lands,
This blessed plot, this earth, this realm, this
    England,
This nurse, this teeming womb of royal
    kings,
Feared by their breed, and famous by their
    birth,
Renownèd for their deeds as far from home,
For Christian service [the crusades]
    and true chivalry,
As is the sepulcher in stubborn Jewry
Of the world's ransom, blessed Mary's son,
This land of such dear souls, this dear dear
    land –
Dear for her reputation through the world
–
Is now leased out – I die pronouncing it –
Like to a tenement [something leased or
    hired] or pelting [insignificant] farm.

31

The Globe

During 1597-8 the **Lord Chamberlain's** Men performed wherever they could find a suitable venue. Eventually, they came up with an inventive plan for a permanent new **playhouse**. In January 1599 workmen dismantled the old Theatre, carried its timbers across the Thames and re-erected them in Southwark as the Globe.

The Globe, recently rebuilt near its original site, is the theatre most closely associated with William Shakespeare. It saw the first performances of all the works of his maturity. Tragically, in 1613 it was accidentally burned down during a performance of *Henry VIII*.

Polygonal in shape, about 20 metres tall and 30 wide, the Globe surrounded an open courtyard into which projected the stage. The canopy above was 'the heavens' while a trapdoor led to 'hell'. Behind the stage actors prepared in a 'tiring house' which had a gallery for musicians at the front. Some three thousand people packed into the Globe, the '**groundlings**' in the yard and the better off in more expensive, covered seats.

The Globe Theatre on the southern bank of the River Thames. It was burned down in 1613, and a modern reconstruction was opened near the original site in 1996.

The house with a thatched roof

Thomas Platter, a young Swiss visitor to London, has left us one of the most detailed accounts of the London theatre scene in 1599.

On September 21st after lunch, about 2 o'clock, I and my party crossed the water, and there in the house with a thatched roof [the Globe, which had such a roof] witnessed an excellent performance of the tragedy of the first Emperor Julius Caesar with a cast of some fifteen people; when the play was over, they danced very marvellously and gracefully together as is their wont, two dressed as men and two as women... [women and girls did not appear in stage plays; their parts were played by men and boys].

Thus daily at two in the afternoon, London has two, sometimes three plays running in different places, competing with each other, and those which play best obtain most spectators. The playhouses are so constructed that they play on a raised platform, so that everyone has a good view. There are different galleries and places, however, where the seating is better and more comfortable and therefore more expensive. For whoever cares to stand below only pays one English penny, but if he wishes to sit he enters by another door, and pays another penny, while if he desires to sit in the most comfortable seats which are cushioned, where he not only sees everything well, but can also be seen [the theatre was a fashionable place to show off one's finery], then he pays yet another English penny at another door. And during the performance food and drink are carried round the **audience**, so that for what one cares to pay one may also have refreshment.

The master

Secure in the new Globe theatre, the **Lord Chamberlain's** Men flourished. They had London's best theatre, best actor (Burbage) and undoubtedly its best playwright. William confirmed his position as England's – perhaps Europe's – leading **dramatist** with a series of masterpieces.

He concluded his second series of history plays (*Richard II* and two parts of *Henry IV*, 1597-1601) with *Henry V* (1599), a stirring exploration of patriotism. There were two more plays set in classical times, *Julius Caesar* and *Troilus and Cressida* (1602). As well as three sparkling comedies – *Much Ado About Nothing* (1598-9), *As You Like It* (1600-1) and *Twelfth Night* (1599-1600) – he wrote what many believe is his finest work, *Hamlet* (1600-2).

RICHARD BURBADGE.
The first Performer of King Richard III.
From an original Picture in Dulwich College.

William had made playwriting an art. He had also established the form in which he mostly wrote (iambic pentameters: lines of ten syllables with alternate weak and strong stress, as in *Richard III*'s 'A horse! A horse! My kingdom for a horse!') as the dominant English **verse** form.

The founder of the Globe: Richard Burbage, actor, businessman and friend of William Shakespeare. This picture was engraved long after his death.

Hamlet's Instructions

William revealed his love of the theatre in the way he introduced '**players**' to perform a play within a play in *Hamlet*. Furthermore, in Prince Hamlet's instructions to the actors (in prose), William almost certainly revealed his own views on good and bad acting.

Speak the speech, I pray you, as I pronounced it to you, trippingly on the tongue. But if you mouth it, as so many of our players do, I had as lief [rather] the town crier spoke my lines. Nor do not saw the air too much with your hand, thus, but use all gently, for in the very torrent, tempest, and (as I may say) whirlwind of your passion, you must acquire and beget [produce] a temperance that may give it smoothness. O, it offends me to the soul to hear a robustious periwig-pated [wearing a wig] fellow tear a passion to tatters, to very rags, to split the ears of the **groundlings**, who for the most part are capable of nothing but inexplicable dumb shows and noise. I would have such a fellow whipped for o'erdoing Termagant. It out-herods Herod [references to parts that were traditionally played with great noise and energy]. Pray you avoid it...

Be not too tame neither, but let your own discretion be your tutor. Suit the action to the word, the word to the action, with this special observance, that you o'erstep not the modesty of nature. For anything so o'erdone is from [beyond, outside] the purpose of playing, whose end, both at the first and now, was and is, to hold, as 'twere, the mirror up to nature.

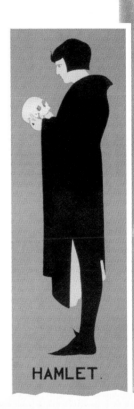

HAMLET.

Ancient into modern: a poster for an 1894 production of *Hamlet* issued by the Beggarstaff Brothers.

The gentleman

From time to time William rode back to Stratford to see his family. Their fortunes were mixed. Hamnet, William and Anne's only son, died in 1596 and John Shakespeare in 1601. However, the Shakespeare girls, Susanna and Judith, grew up to marry into respectable Stratford families.

By the mid-1590s William had money to spend. It came principally from his position as a **shareholder** in the **Lord Chamberlain's** Men. Shareholders invested their talents and some money in the company, and in return shared its profits. Playing to **audiences** of 3000 people, each paying at least a penny, William's company made a good deal of profit.

As a mark of his new status, in 1596 William was granted a **coat of arms**, making him officially a gentleman (a rank in society between common people and the nobility). The next year he bought New Place, the second-largest house in Stratford. He invested £320 in land near Stratford in 1602 and a further £440 in 1605. By 1612, when he bought a house in London, near Blackfriars, he was a wealthy man.

Genius in middle age? A head and shoulders portrait of the English playwright.

On the road
Some idea of the comforts William experienced on his trips to and from Stratford can be gained from these words on English inns in the *Itinerary* (1617) of Fynes Moryson (1566–c.1617).

The World affords no such inns as England hath, either for good and cheap entertainment after the Guests' own pleasure, or for humble attendance on passengers; yea, even in very poor villages ... For as soon as a passenger comes to an Inn, the servants run to him, and one takes his horse, and walks him till he be cold, then rubs him and gives him meat [food], yet I must say that they are not much to be trusted in this last point, without the eye of the Master or his servant to observe them. Another servant gives the passenger his private chamber, and kindles his fire; the third pulls off his boots, and makes them clean. Then the Host or Hostess visit him; and if he will eat with the host, or at a common table with others, his meal will cost him six pence, or in some places but four pence (yet this course is less honourable and not used by Gentlemen); but if he will eat in his chamber, he commands what meat he will, according to his appetite ... and when he sits at table, the Host or Hostess will accompany him, or if they have many guests, will at least visit him...

New reign, new opportunities

Elizabeth's long reign ended with her death in 1603. In her last decade, war and economic difficulties had somewhat tarnished her bright image, and the new monarch, her cousin James VI of Scotland, was welcomed with much rejoicing.

The king, reigning in England as James I (1603-25), was well-educated and intelligent, with a delight in **revelry**. Compared with Scotland, where he had ruled in some discomfort for 26 years, England was a land of glorious riches – and he was eager to spend. The court became, after years of penny-pinching, a fountain of riches, reward and extravagant artistic enterprise. Among those who benefited was William Shakespeare.

James wished to see his court adorned with the finest: the best painters, musicians, designers and theatre companies. Hence his patronage of the King's Men (see page 26). Their court performances continued and, as we shall see, the company's chief playwright responded to James' patronage with a play to suit every royal taste.

King of two kingdoms: James I of England and VI of Scotland, who took over **patronage** of Shakespeare's theatre company in 1603.

The state of monarchy

Puritans mocked the contrast between King James' high-minded pronouncements, and his person and behaviour. This is illustrated in these extracts. The first is from one of the king's lectures on monarchy. The second is an unkind sketch of James (published after he was dead) by a disappointed ex-courtier.

1. *The state of monarchy is the supremest thing upon earth. For kings are not only God's lieutenants upon earth, and sit upon God's throne, but even by God himself they are called gods. There be three principal similitudes [similarities] that illustrate the state of monarchy. One taken from the word of God, and the two other out of the grounds of policy and philosophy. In the Scriptures kings are called gods ... Kings are also compared to fathers of families, for a king is truly ... the politic father of his people. And lastly, kings are compared to the head of ... the body of man.*

2. *He was of middle stature, more corpulent through his clothes than in his body, yet fat enough, his clothes ever being made large and easy, the doublets [types of jacket] quilted for stiletto [thin-bladed knife] proof, his breeches in great pleats and full stuffed. He was naturally of a timorous [timid or frightened] disposition, which was the reason for, his quilted doublets; his eyes large, ever rolling after any stranger came into his presence... His beard was very thin, his tongue too large for his mouth, which ever made him speak full in the mouth, and made him drink very uncomely [unattractive], as if eating his drink, which came out into the cup of each side of his mouth.*

Everybody had their place in society. This picture of an Elizabethan family suggests that the wife and children must obey the father.

A play for the King

King James wielded immense power. Many – including the King himself – believed he had been appointed to the throne by God. The superstitious said his touch could cure diseases. He could declare war, make peace, raise men to wealth and importance overnight – and just as swiftly bring them down again.

It was vital, therefore, that the King's Men please their **patron**. To this end, probably towards the end of 1605, William wrote *Macbeth*. He set the play in Scotland, the land of the King's birth. Moreover, as all kings were proud of their ancient ancestry, in Act IV, scene i, he demonstrated how James was descended from Banquo, an ancient Scottish hero.

James considered himself an expert on witchcraft. To please him further, the playwright created *Macbeth's* witches, who start the play with the famous lines, 'When shall we three meet again?' James certainly liked the play and it was probably first performed at court before his Danish brother-in-law, King Christian.

The murderous pair, Lady Macbeth (Francesca Annis) and her husband (Jon Finch) in Roman Polanski's film of *Macbeth* (1971).

Royal frolics

Sir John Harrington (1561-1612), a godson of Elizabeth I, has left us an amusing account of the court revels that marked the visit of King Christian of Denmark in 1606. It was in this sort of atmosphere that *Macbeth* was first performed.

One day a great feast was held, and after dinner the representation of Solomon, his temple, and the coming of the Queen of Sheba was made, or (as I may say) was meant to have been made, before their Majesties. But, alas! as all earthly things do fail poor mortals in enjoyment, so did prove the presentment [showing] hereof. The lady who did play the queen's part did carry most precious gifts to both their majesties; but forgetting the steps arising to the canopy, overset her caskets into his Danish Majesty's lap and fell at his feet, though I rather think it was in his face. Much was the hurry and confusion; cloths and napkins were at hand, to make all clean. His Majesty then got up and would dance with the Queen of Sheba; but he fell down and humbled himself before her, and was carried to an inner chamber and laid on a bed of state; which was not a little defiled with the presents of the queen which had been bestowed upon his garments; such as wine, cream, jelly, beverage, cakes, spices, and other good matters. The entertainment and show went forward, and most of the presenters went backward, or fell down, wine did so occupy their upper chambers [their brains].

Rich and famous

By 1610, William's literary successes, wise investments and links with the court had made him rich and famous. Interestingly, the tone of his dramas does not reflect his worldly success.

From about 1600 his work entered the sombre phase in which he wrote his great tragedies: *Hamlet*, *Othello* (1604), *Macbeth*, *King Lear* (1605-6) and *Antony and Cleopatra* (1606-7). The so-called 'comedies' of this time – *All's Well that Ends Well* (1603) and *Measure for Measure* (about 1604) – are also marked with darkness.

Between about 1607 and his death in 1616, William wrote less. His work reflects yet another mood, too. *Pericles* (1608-9), *Cymbeline* (1609-10), *The Winter's Tale* (1610-11) and *The Tempest* (1611) do not fit easily into the traditional categories. They are experimental, mixing fantasy with reality, tragedy with comedy.

Many reasons for the change have been suggested, including the death of William's mother (1608). More likely, he felt he had exhausted the traditional styles of drama and wanted to break into new territory.

Real-life husband and wife, Laurence Olivier and Vivien Leigh in *Antony and Cleopatra*, **1951.**

A tale of jealousy – Laurence Fishburne (as Othello, left) and Kenneth Branagh (as Iago) in Shakespeare's tragedy, *Othello*.

Fire!

In 1612–13 William worked with John Fletcher (1579–1625) on *Henry VIII*. As Henry Wotton recorded in 1613, the play's elaborate sound effects included a cannon, which proved the death-knell of the Globe **playhouse**.

The king's **Players** had a new Play, called All Is True, representing some principal pieces of the reign of Henry the 8th, which was set forth with many extraordinary Circumstances of Pomp and Majesty, even to the matting of the stage; the Knights of the Order, with their Georges and Garter [knights were, and still are, divided into 'orders', such as the Knights of St George and the Order of the Garter], the Guards with their embroidered coats, and the like: sufficient in truth within a while to make Greatness very familiar, if not ridiculous. Now, King Henry was making a masque [a type of elaborate drama in which the spectacular staging, music and so forth were of great importance] at the Cardinal Wolsey's House, and certain Cannons being shot of[f] at his entry, some of the Paper, or other stuff, wherewith one of them was stopped, did light the Thatch, where being thought at first but an idle smoak, and their Eyes more attentive to the show, it kindled inwardly, and ran round like a train, consuming within less than an hour the whole House to the very ground.

The new world

One of William's last plays, *The Tempest*, takes place on a remote and mysterious island. This setting is highly significant. It reflects the thrill Europeans felt as contact was made with hitherto unknown parts of the world.

The process began in the fifteenth century. Christopher Columbus took the most important step when he sailed from Spain to the Americas in 1492. Thirty years later Sebastian del Cano completed the first round-the-world voyage, begun under the leadership of Ferdinand Magellan. Under Elizabeth I, Francis Drake also **circumnavigated** the globe and Sir Walter Raleigh attempted to found English **colonies** in North America.

In 1607 a permanent English colony was established in the New World. England was now no longer at the edge of the known world, but in its centre. Beyond its shores lay uncounted peoples, cultures, religions and creatures.

As the **Reformation** had overturned religious certainties, so the explorations overturned geographical certainties. It was all, as said Prospero in *The Tempest*, 'such stuff as dreams are made on.'

Arise, Sir Francis! A famous but fanciful painting of Queen Elizabeth knighting Francis Drake in 1581 after his epic round-the-world voyage.

A little round light
In 1609 Sir Thomas Gates was shipwrecked on the Bermudas. William read a manuscript account of his troubles in the summer of 1610 and used it as a source for *The Tempest*.

During all this time, the heavens looked so black upon us, that it was not possible the elevation of the Pole [Pole (North) Star] might be observed: nor a star by night, nor sun beam by day was to be seen. Only upon the Thursday night Sir George Summers, being upon the watch [lookout], had an apparition of a little round light, like a feint star, trembling, and streaming along with a sparkling blaze, half the height of the mainmast, and shooting sometimes from shroud [part of the ship's rigging] to shroud; ... and for three or four hours together, or rather more, half the night it kept with us, running sometimes along the main-yard [main cross-beam upon which the sail hung] to the very end, and then returning. At which, Sir George Summers called divers [various (people)] about him, and showed them the same, who observed it with much wonder, and carefulness: but upon a sudden, towards the morning watch, they lost the sight of it, and knew not what way it made. ... But it did not light us any whit the more to our known way, who ran now (as do hoodwinked [blindfolded] men) at all adventures, sometimes north, and northeast, then north and by west... [until] Sir George Summers, when no man dreamed of such happiness, had discovered and cried 'Land.'

'cursed be he...'

The Victorians believed a creative person should have their head in the clouds and be unworldly. Consequently, William perplexed them: he was both a brilliant writer and a most successful businessman. The combination of art and business seemed to the Victorians most unusual.

Nowadays, in an age where actors, singers and writers are commonly millionaires, we can more easily accept William's varied talents. All he did was apply his intelligence to everything he did, making both plays and money.

William's playwriting, therefore, was a means of making money. By the second decade of the seventeenth century, he was well off and had probably said all he wished to say.

There was nothing unusual in William's retirement after 1613. By the standards of the day he was getting old: his brother Gilbert had died in 1612 and Richard was buried the following year. By the spring of 1616 William, too, felt the end was near.

In March he made his will. He saw that his daughter Judith would not be left penniless by her dubious husband, Thomas Quiney. Most went to his other daughter Susanna and her doctor husband. Intriguingly, to Anne Shakespeare he bequeathed very little indeed.

William Shakespeare died on 23 April, perhaps of a fever caught after a drinking bout with his old pals Ben Jonson and Michael Drayton. He was buried in Holy Trinity, Stratford, beneath a stone slab with the following inscription:

Good friend for Jesus' sake forebear
To dig the dust enclosed here;
Blessed be the man that spares these stones
*And cursed be he that moves my bones.**

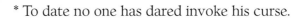

* To date no one has dared invoke his curse.

I, William Shakespeare

William's will, dated 25 March 1616, is the fullest **document** about him that we have from his own lifetime.

I William Shakespeare, of Stratford upon Avon in the county of Warr., gent., in perfect health and memory, God be praised, do make and ordain this my last will and testament in manner and form following...

Item, I give and bequeath unto my daughter Judith one hundred and fifty pounds of lawful English money...
Item, I give and bequeath unto my said sister Joan £20 and all my wearing apparel...
Item, I give and bequeath unto her three sons, William Hart, – Hart, and Michael Hart, five pounds apiece...
Item, I give and bequeath unto the said Elizabeth Hall all my plate (except my broad silver and gilt bowl)...
Item, I give and bequeath unto the poor of Stratford aforesaid ten pounds; to Mr Thomas Combe my sword...
Item, I give, will, bequeath and devise unto my daughter Susanna Hall ... New Place...
Item, I give unto my wife my second best bed with the furniture.
Item, I give and bequeath to my said daughter Judith my broad silver gilt bowl.
All the rest of my goods, chattels, leases, plate, jewels, and household stuff whatsoever ... I give, devise and bequeath to my son-in-law, John Hall, gent., and my daughter Susanna his wife...

Soul of the age

It is not easy to know precisely what William wrote. We have, perhaps, only one section of a play – *Sir Thomas More* (c.1593-c.1601) – in his own handwriting. Even this is not certain. Like several other plays, he had worked on this one with other **dramatists**.

When William died, only his poetry and fourteen of his plays had been printed. The texts were full of printer's errors. Moreover, the material that the printers had reproduced was itself flawed: actors had often altered or only half-remembered the playwright's hand-written scripts.

To keep his work available, a group of William's contemporaries assembled copies of all his plays and published them in what is called the *First Folio* (1623). There were differences, of course between these and earlier texts, and scholars have been labouring ever since to discover the 'true' texts. Whatever they come up with, one thing remains the same: William's plays continue to delight **audiences** just as they did during his lifetime.

Fellow playwright and great admirer of William Shakespeare, Ben Jonson is buried in Westminster Abbey.

Jonson's praise

Ben Jonson (1572–1637) marked the death of William Shakespeare, fellow playwright and friend, with the poem, *To the Memory of my Beloved Master William Shakespeare, and What he Hath Left Us*. In the last ten lines he says that William's works shine on after his death like a new constellation of stars.

To draw no envy, SHAKESPEARE, on thy name,
Am I thus ample to thy book and fame;
While I confess thy writings to be such,
As neither Man nor Muse [an inspiring goddess] *can praise too much...*
I therefore will begin: Soul of the age!
The applause! Delight! The wonder of our stage!
My SHAKESPEARE rise! I will not lodge thee by
Chaucer [Geoffrey Chaucer (c.1345–1400), the first great poet of the
     English language], *or Spenser* [Edmund Spenser (c.1552–99), a fine
     Elizabethan poet], *or bid Beaumont* [Francis Beaumont (c.1584–1616),
     a respected early Jacobean playwright] *lie*
A little further, to make thee a room:
Thou art a monument without a tomb,
And art alive still while thy book doth live
And we have wits to read, and praise to give ...
Sweet Swan of Avon ! what a sight it were
To see thee in our waters yet appear,
And make those flights upon the banks of Thames [the river that runs
     through London, see p. 20],
That so did take Eliza, and our James! [Queen Elizabeth I and King James I,
     see pp. 10 and 28]
But stay, I see thee in the hemisphere
Advanced, and made a constellation there !
Shine forth, thou Star of Poets, and with rage
Or influence, chide [criticize] *or cheer the drooping stage,*
Which, since thy flight from hence, hath mourned like night,
And despairs day, but for thy volume's light.

A golden age?

The English used to talk of the reign of Elizabeth I as a 'golden age'. They pointed to the country's growing wealth, confidence and importance, its explorers, the defeat of the Spanish Armada, the majesty of the Queen herself and, of course, a glorious literature crowned by the works of William Shakespeare. Today we are less sure. How can the age be described as golden when the majority lived on the edge of starvation, when torture and cruelty were commonplace, when the expectation of life at birth was about thirty, when women – half the population – were subject to mindless discrimination and ill-treatment?

No, the age of Elizabeth was not golden, certainly not for the nameless masses whose lives were short, crude and brutal. Yet there was a golden glow. It was provided by William Shakespeare, the genius who took a young language and a young art form, and created from them art that will probably endure as long as civilization itself.

The old city of London, with the medieval St Paul's Cathedral at its heart, as it appeared before the Great Fire of 1666 destroyed a good part of it.

References
1 S.ᵗ Pauls
2 S.ᵗ Dunstans
3 Temple
4 S.ᵗ Brides
5 S.ᵗ Andrews
6 Baynards Castle
7 S.ᵗ Sepulchres
8 Bow Church
9 Guild-hall
10 S.ᵗ Michaels
11 S.ᵗ Laurence Poultney
12 Old Swan

A View of LONDON as it appeared before the dreadful-Fire in 1666.

13 London Bridge
14 S.ᵗ Dunstans East
15 Billingsgate
16 Custom house
17 Tower
18 Dᵉ Wharf
19 S.ᵗ Olaves
20 S.ᵗ Mary overn
21 Winchester-house
22 The Globe
23 The Bear Garden
24 Hampstead
25 Highgate
26 Hackney

All the world's a stage

The last word must go to William himself. In one of his most famous passages, from *As You Like It*, he has the world-weary Jaques, using the image of the theatre, sum up the human condition in words that still delight and fascinate.

All the world's a stage,
And all the men and women merely **players**;
They have their exits and their entrances,
And one man in his time plays many parts,
His acts being seven ages. At first, the infant,
Mewling and puking in the nurse's arms.
Then the whining schoolboy, with his satchel
And shining morning face, creeping like a snail
Unwillingly to school. And then the lover,
Sighing like a furnace, with a woeful ballad
Made to his mistress' eyebrow. Then a soldier,
Full of strange oaths and bearded like the pard [leopard],
Jealous in honour, sudden and quick in quarrel,
Seeking the bubble reputation
Even in the cannon's mouth. And then the justice,
In fair round belly with good capon lined,
With eyes severe and beard of formal cut,
Full of wise saws [sayings] and modern instances
    [examples];
And so he plays his part. The sixth age shifts
Into the lean and slippered pantaloon,
With spectacles on nose and pouch on side;
His youthful hose [tights, leg coverings], well saved, a world
    too wide
For his shrunk shank [leg], and his big manly voice,
Turning again toward childish treble, pipes
And whistles in his sound. Last scene of all,
In this strange eventful history,
Is second childishness and mere oblivion,
Sans [without] teeth, sans eyes, sans taste, sans everything.

51

Timeline

1558	Elizabeth I becomes Queen of England
1559	Protestant Church of England is re-founded
1564	William Shakespeare is born in Stratford-upon-Avon
1576	The Theatre (**playhouse**) is built in north London
1577-81	Francis Drake **circumnavigates** the globe
1582	Shakespeare marries Anne Hathaway
1583	Susanna Shakespeare is born
1585	Hamnet and Judith Shakespeare (twins) are born
1587	The Rose (playhouse) is built in Southwark
1588-90	Shakespeare comes to London about this time
1593-4	London theatres closed due to outbreak of plague
1594	First play is printed – *Titus Andronicus*
	Shakespeare joins Burbage to form the **Lord Chamberlain's** Men
1599	The Theatre reopens as the Globe in Southwark
1601	John Shakespeare dies
1603	Elizabeth I dies. James VI of Scotland becomes James I of England
	Lord Chamberlain's Men become King's Men
1608	King's Men start using Blackfriars indoor playhouse
1609	*The Sonnets* are published
1612	Gilbert Shakespeare (brother) dies
1613	Richard Shakespeare (brother) dies
	Globe Theatre is burned down
1616	William Shakespeare dies
1623	*First Folio* edition of plays is published
1709	Nicholas Rowe's carefully edited works of Shakespeare and the first biography of the playwright are published
1996	Globe Theatre opens near its old site in Southwark

Find out more

Books and websites

Shakespeare, Wendy Greenhill, Paul Wignall, (Heinemann Library, 2000).
Shakespeare's Theatre, Wendy Greenhill, (Heinemann Library, 2000).
The Life and World of Shakespeare, Struan Reid, (Heinemann Library, 2001).

Go Exploring! Log on to Heinemann's online history resource at
www.heinemannexplore.co.uk

www.shakespeare.org.uk
This site contains material about all aspects of Shakespeare's life.

List of primary sources

The author and publisher gratefully acknowledge the following publications and websites from which written sources in the book are drawn. In some cases the wording or sentence structure has been simplified to make the material more appropriate for a school readership.

P.9 (top) Reprinted in G.B. Harrison, *Introducing Shakespeare*, 3rd Edition, (Penguin, 1966) p. 39.

P.9 (bottom) Sir Thomas Wilson, *The State of England*, 1600, F.J. Fisher, ed., (The Camden Society, Third Series LII, Miscellany vol.. 16, 1936) p. 19.

P.11 William Harrison, *The Description of England*, Georges Edelen, ed., (The Folger Shakespeare Library, and Dover Publications, 1994) pp. 180–1.

P.13 Oliver Lawson Dick, ed., *Aubrey's Brief Lives*, (Penguin English Library, 1972) p. 437.

P.15 *Foxe's Book of Martyrs*, (James Nisbet, 1891) p. 387.

P.17 Cited in Andrew Gurr, *Playgoing in Shakespeare's London*, 2nd edit., (CUP, 1996) pp. 214–15. Spelling simplified by Stewart Ross.

P.19 Act V, scene ii, lines 144–66. *The Taming of the Shrew*.

P.21 Everyman edition, (J.P. Dent & Sons, 1912) pp. 376-7.

P.23 Cited in G.B. Harrison, *Introducing Shakespeare*, (Pelican, 1966) p. 48.

P.25 Translated by Gottfried von Bülow and cited in Russ McDonald, *The Bedford Companion to Shakespeare*, (St Martin's, 1999) p. 241.

P.27 Cited Andrew Gurr, *The Shakespearean Stage 1574–1642*, 3rd edit., (CUP, 1992) pp. 155–6. Spelling simplified by Stewart Ross.

P.29 G.E. Bentley, *The Jacobean and Caroline Stage*, 7 vols, (OUP, 1941–68) vol. VI, pp. 266–7; cited in Andrew Gurr, *The Shakespearean Stage 1574–1642*, 3rd edition, (CUP, 1992) pp. 203–6.

P.31 *Richard II*, Act II, scene i, lines 31–60.

P.33 *Travels in England*, translated by Clare Williams; cited in Andrew Gurr, Playgoing in *Shakespeare's London*, 2nd edit., (CUP, 1996) p.222.

P.35 *Hamlet*, Act III, scene ii, lines 1–45.

P.37 Cited in A.F. Scott, ed., *The Stuart Age*, (White Lion, 1974) p. 198. Spelling simplified by Stewart Ross.

P.39 1. Speech to Parliament, March 1610, cited in J.P. Kenyon, *The Stuart Constitution*, (CUP, 1966) pp. 12–13.
2. Sir Anthony Weldon, *Court and Character of James I*, 1650, cited in A.F. Scott, ed., *The Stuart Age*, (White Lion, 1974) p. 5.

P.41 A letter from Sir John Harrington (1561–1612) cited in Russ McDonald, *The Bedford Companion* to Shakespeare, (St Martin's, 1996) p. 326.

P.43 Letter to Edmund Bacon, cited in Andrew Gurr, *Playgoing in Shakespeare's London*, 2nd edition, (CUP 1996) p. 235–6.

P.45 Sir William Strachey, *True Reportory of the Wreck and Redemption of Sir Thomas Gates, Knight, upon and from the Islands of the Bermudas*, 1625, cited in Russ McDonald, *The Bedford Companion to Shakespeare*, (St Martin's, 1996) pp. 137–8.

P.47 Cited in G.B. Harrison, *Introducing Shakespeare*, (Pelican, 1966) pp. 69–75.

P.49 Jonson, Ben. *The Works of Ben Jonson*, vol. 3, (Chatto & Windus, 1910) pp. 287–9.

P.51 *As You Like It*, Act II, Scene vii, lines 138–65.

Glossary

allegiance duty to obey and follow someone in a position of power

amateur doing something for love of it, not money

audience either spectators, or a personal meeting with an important person, such as a king or the Pope

bubonic plague killer disease, also known as the Black Death, marked by dark swellings on the body

circumnavigate sail around (the world)

civil servant someone paid to work for the government

coat of arms official symbols representing a family

colony a territory that is owned and governed by another country

compromise an agreement that is reached by settling differences, and by both sides dropping some of their demands

conservative unwilling to change

contemporary of the same time period as something or someone

corporation body governing a city, with a mayor at its head

council body that advised the monarch

document important or official piece of writing

dramatist playwright

Earl title of nobility

edited checked carefully for mistakes

groundlings members of the audience in an Elizabethan theatre who stood or sat on the ground in the theatre's yard

Holy Roman Emperor the most powerful German prince

Lord Chamberlain official responsible for court ceremonies and for keeping an eye on the plays being performed in London's theatres

martyr someone who is killed for their faith

morality play late-medieval verse dramas in which actors played vices (such as 'greed') and virtues (such as 'mercy')

patron someone who uses their money and influence to support others

patron saint saint who is said to protect a country

player actor

playhouse theatre

professional working or done for money

Puritan someone who wanted to make the Church of England more Protestant by removing all traces of Roman Catholicism, such as religious statues

Reformation the split between the Protestant and Roman Catholic churches in the sixteenth century

revelry jollity, partying

shareholder someone who invested talent and money in a theatre company in the hope of making a profit

sonnet poem of fourteen lines

titled having a title, such as 'sir' or 'earl'

troupe performing group

upstart a person who has risen above his previous position in society, without respecting social norms

urban belonging to towns and cities

verse rhyming poetry

Shakespeare's works

A Lover's Complaint
A Midsummer Night's Dream
All's Well That Ends Well
Antony and Cleopatra
As You Like It
The Comedy of Errors
Coriolanus
Cymbeline
Hamlet
Henry IV, part 1
Henry IV, part 2
Henry V
Henry VI, part 1
Henry VI, part 2
Henry VI, part 3
Henry VIII
Julius Caesar
King John
King Lear
Love's Labours Lost
Macbeth
Measure for Measure
The Merchant of Venice

The Merry Wives of Windsor
Much Ado About Nothing
Othello
Pericles, Prince of Tyre
The Rape of Lucrece
Richard II
Richard III
Romeo and Juliet
The Sonnets
The Taming of the Shrew
The Tempest
Timon of Athens
Titus Andronicus
Troilus and Cressida
Twelfth Night
The Two Gentlemen of Verona
Venus and Adonis
The Winter's Tale

**Other plays to which
Shakespeare contributed**
The Two Noble Kinsmen
Sir Thomas More

Index